Exploring English
GRAMMAR

Continental

Credits

Illustrations: Denny Bond, Murray Callahan, Laurie Conley, Doris Ettlinger, Estella Hickman, Matt LeBarre, Eva Vagreti, Rob Williams

ISBN 978-1-5240-0265-7

Table of Contents

Introduction to
Exploring English Grammar

You use language every day to speak, listen, read, and write. Using language effectively helps you to communicate your thoughts and ideas to those around you. To understand and use the English language, you must understand and use the rules of grammar. Knowing parts of speech, punctuation, sentence structure, and capitalization rules helps you to master the English language. *Exploring English Grammar* reviews important language rules to help you grow into a skillful communicator.

Exploring English Grammar includes skills in the following areas:

- Sentence structure
- Nouns
- Verbs
- Verb tenses
- Pronouns
- Adjectives
- Adverbs
- Types of sentences
- Capitalization
- Punctuation
- Word usage
- Letter writing

UNIT 1: Sentences

Sentences and Fragments

Remember   A **sentence** is a group of words that tells a complete thought. If the words do not tell a complete thought, they are a **fragment.**

Sentence   Hummingbirds drink with their tongues.

Fragment   Juice from flowers.

Sentence   They seem to hang in the air.

Fragment   Fly fast.

Think About   Look at the sentences. Look at the fragments. What is the difference?

_____

_____

_____

Read and Apply   Read the groups of words. Write **S** over each group of words that is a sentence. Write **F** over each group of words that is a fragment.

The smallest bird in the world. Hummingbirds zoom

around quickly. Their wings make a humming sound.

This sound gave them their name. Lays just two eggs.

The tiny eggs are the size of beans. With its long bill.

Hummingbirds like to eat bugs.

Write About

Find each group of words that you marked **F** for fragment in Read and Apply. Add words to the group to make it a sentence. Tell a complete thought. Write the complete sentences below.

_____

_____

_____

_____

_____

_____

_____

Review

Listen to each group of words. Circle **SENTENCE** or **FRAGMENT** to describe each group.

1.   SENTENCE   FRAGMENT

2.   SENTENCE   FRAGMENT

3.   SENTENCE   FRAGMENT

4.   SENTENCE   FRAGMENT

5.   SENTENCE   FRAGMENT

Subject Part

Remember Every sentence has two parts. The **subject** tells who or what the sentence is about. The subject can be just one word. It can also be a group of words.

<u>Many bright stars</u> fill the night sky.

<u>They</u> sometimes look like animals or things.

<u>Powerful telescopes</u> help us to see the stars.

Think About Look at the underlined words above. How can you tell that these words are subjects? What do they tell you?

_____

_____

_____

Read and Apply Read the sentences. Draw a line under the subject part of each sentence.

Constellations are groups of stars. Early people told

stories about the stars. They looked for pictures in the stars.

Orion the Hunter is one of the largest constellations. Three

bright stars make up Orion's belt. These stars are in a row.

Maps of the stars show Orion and other constellations.

Write About   Write about something you like to do outside at night. Write at least four sentences. Underline the subject part of each sentence.

_____

_____

_____

_____

_____

_____

Review   Add a subject part to complete each sentence below. Write words from the box or think of your own.

Scientists	The night sky	The North Star	Many people

1. _____ like to look at the stars.

2. _____ is full of beautiful sights.

3. _____ study the stars and planets.

4. _____ helped early sailors.

Predicate Part

Remember   Every sentence has two parts. The **predicate** tells what the subject does or is. The predicate can be just one word. It can also be a group of words.

The Erie Canal <u>is in New York State</u>.

The water <u>flows</u>.

Mules <u>helped to move barges</u>.

Think About   Look at the underlined words above. How can you tell that these words are predicates? What do they tell you?

_____

_____

_____

Read and Apply   Read the sentences. Draw a line under the predicate part of each sentence.

Workers finished the Erie Canal in 1825. Lake Erie was its starting point. The Erie Canal crossed New York State to the Hudson River. It stretched out 363 miles. Ships on the Erie Canal carried wood and food to the East. People traveled west to new homes. The Erie Canal made getting places easier.

Write About   Write about a big job you have finished. Write at least four sentences. Underline the predicate part of each sentence.

_____

_____

_____

_____

_____

Review   Add a predicate part to complete each sentence below. Write words from the box or think of your own.

couldn't use it	made the canal deeper
pulled the boats	was once only 4 feet deep

1. The Erie Canal _____.

2. Big ships _____.

3. Workers in 1909 _____.

4. Teams of mules _____.

11

Statements and Questions

Remember A **statement** is a sentence that tells about something. It ends with a **period (.)**. A **question** is a sentence that asks about something. It ends with a **question mark (?)**.

Statement Jazz music started in the United States.

Question Was jazz music popular?

Word order is different in statements and questions. A helping verb goes before the subject in some questions.

Statement You can play the piano.

Question Can you play the piano?

Think About When do you use a statement? When do you use a question?

_____

_____

_____

Read and Apply Read the sentences. Write **S** above each sentence that is a statement. Write **Q** above each sentence that is a question.

There are many types of jazz music. Some jazz music is fast. Can you dance to jazz? There are special dances you can do. What instruments are played in jazz? Jazz uses trumpets, pianos, and saxophones. Are there any other instruments? Jazz music also uses clarinets and drums. Who are some famous jazz musicians? Billie Holiday was a famous jazz singer. Louis Armstrong was also a jazz musician.

12

Write About   Write three statements about your favorite type of music, a famous musician, or your favorite band.

_____

_____

_____

_____

Write three questions you would like to ask a famous musician.

_____

_____

_____

Review   Change the word order. Make each statement into a question. Make each question into a statement.

1. You can dance to jazz music.

_____

2. Has jazz been around since the 1920s?

_____

3. Was bebop a type of jazz music?

_____

4. Vicky will sing this song.

_____

Question Words

Remember Most questions use **question words.** Who, what, when, and where are question words.

Who plays the piano?
Troy plays the piano.

Where is the milk?
The milk is on the table.

What color is the hat?
The hat is blue.

When is the picnic?
The picnic is at 2:00.

Think About The question word what asks about events or things. What do the question words who, when, and where ask about?

_____

_____

_____

Read and Apply Read the sentences. Put a line under each question word.

Mia said, "What time does the play start? Where are we going to see it?"

Carter answered, "It starts at 6:30. The play is at the Old Theater on Main Street. When do you want to meet?"

Mia said, "Let's meet at 5:30. Where should we meet?"

Carter answered, "We can meet at my house."

Mia said, "Who is playing the main part in the play?"

Carter said, "I think Rick Mason is playing the part."

14

Write About Pretend you are going to have the chance to ask a famous person some questions. Write six questions you want to ask. Use the question words <u>who</u>, <u>what</u>, <u>when</u>, or <u>where</u>. Write at least one question with each word.

_____

_____

_____

_____

_____

_____

_____

Review Read each sentence. Then write a question about the facts in it. Begin your sentence with <u>who</u>, <u>what</u>, <u>when</u>, or <u>where</u>.

1. Elvis Presley was a famous singer.

_____

2. He sang rock and roll music.

_____

3. He traveled all over the world.

_____

4. Elvis Presley died in 1977.

_____

Commands and Exclamations

Remember   A **command** is a sentence that asks or tells someone to do something. It usually ends with a **period (.).** An **exclamation** is a sentence that shows surprise or strong feeling. It ends with an **exclamation point (!).**

Command   Work the clay with your fingers.
Add water to keep it soft.

Exclamation   Great job!
That looks wonderful!

Think About   When might you use a command? When might you use an exclamation?

_____

_____

_____

Read and Apply   Read the sentences. Circle each sentence that is a command. Draw a line under each sentence that is an exclamation. Some sentences are neither type of sentence.

Do you want to make a clay pot? Break off a large chunk of

clay. Roll it into a long, thin rope. It must be even! This is tricky!

Curl the clay tightly into a circle. Now you have the bottom of

the pot. Start the sides next.

Write About Write three commands. Tell what to do next to finish the clay pot.

_____

_____

_____

_____

Write three exclamations. Tell something special you might say after finishing the clay pot.

_____

_____

_____

_____

Review Listen to the sentences. Circle **COMMAND** or **EXCLAMATION** for each sentence.

1. COMMAND   EXCLAMATION

2. COMMAND   EXCLAMATION

3. COMMAND   EXCLAMATION

4. COMMAND   EXCLAMATION

5. COMMAND   EXCLAMATION

Run-On Sentences

Remember   A **sentence** tells a complete thought. If two or more thoughts get run together, the group of words is not a sentence. It is a **run-on sentence.**

Run-on   US coins are different sizes dimes are the smallest.

Sentences   US coins are different sizes. Dimes are the smallest.

Think About   How can you fix a run-on sentence?

_____

_____

Read and Apply   Read this paragraph. Draw a line under the run-on sentences.

Many people like to collect coins. Some coins are very rare there are not many of them left. These coins might be worth a lot of money. One rare coin is called the Brasher Doubloon it is named after a man who made it. It was made in 1786 there are only a few of these coins. One coin sold for more than $4 million!

Write About   Read each run-on sentence. Then write it correctly. Use end punctuation and a capital letter to separate the sentences.

1. Before 1934, our country had a gold coin worth ten dollars it was called an eagle. _____

_____

2. Other countries also have interesting money have you ever seen any?

_____

_____

3. A Japanese yen has a dragon on its face how fierce it looks!

_____

_____

4. Save any old coins that you find they can be worth collecting.

_____

_____

Review   Look at each run-on sentence. Draw a line to show where to separate it to make it two sentences.

1. Countries around the world use different types of money most countries in Europe use the euro.

2. Money can be bills or coins bills are made of paper.

3. Some countries' money is very colorful the bills show pictures of famous people.

UNIT 2: Nouns

Nouns

Remember   A **noun** names a person, place, animal, or thing.

People	doctor	sisters	Tyler
Animals	beaver	hens	Jasper
Places	park	towns	Montana
Things	tree	apples	*Titanic*

Think About   Look around you. What are some nouns you see?

_____

_____

_____

Read and Apply   Read this paragraph. Put a line under each noun.

Mary Anning grew up in a small town in England. The young girl looked for old bones along the beaches there. Mary and her brother found the skeleton of a dinosaur. Later, she found many more fossils and bones of creatures. Scientists all over the world now study their skeletons.

Write About   Write a paragraph telling about finding something you had lost.
Then circle all the nouns in your paragraph.

_____

_____

_____

_____

_____

_____

_____

_____

Review   Listen to each word. Circle **NOUN** if the word is a noun. Circle
NOT A NOUN if the word is not a noun.

1.   NOUN   NOT A NOUN

2.   NOUN   NOT A NOUN

3.   NOUN   NOT A NOUN

4.   NOUN   NOT A NOUN

5.   NOUN   NOT A NOUN

21

Common and Proper Nouns

Remember A **common noun** names any person, place, animal, or thing. A **proper noun** names a special person, place, animal, or thing.

Common	girl	city	dog	month
Proper	Sarah	Dallas	Fido	October

Think About Look at the examples of common and proper nouns. How are they different?

_____

_____

Read and Apply Read these paragraphs. Put a line under each common noun. Circle each proper noun.

Some scientists study space. At first, they could only study it from Earth. Then people began to go to space. Russia and America were the first countries to send up rockets. Scientists learned a lot from Laika, a dog, and Abe, a chimp.

Yuri Gagarin and John Glenn were the first men to circle our planet. Later, Sally Ride was the first woman to go into space. She traveled on the _Challenger._

22

Write About Write a paragraph telling about some place you visited with a friend or a family member. Use proper nouns in your paragraph.

_____

_____

_____

_____

_____

_____

_____

Review Write a common noun to tell what each proper noun is. Write a proper noun as an example of each common noun.

1. _Mayflower_ _____

2. Florida _____

3. Clara Barton _____

4. July _____

5. France _____

6. singer _____

7. city _____

8. school _____

9. day _____

10. cat _____

Singular and Plural Nouns

Remember   A **singular noun** names one person, place, animal, or thing. A **plural noun** names more than one.

Add **s** to most nouns to make them plural.

car ➡ car<u>s</u>

Add **es** to nouns that end in **s, x, ch,** or **sh.**

brush ➡ brush<u>es</u>   box ➡ box<u>es</u>

Drop the **y** and add **ies** to nouns that end in **y.**

lady ➡ lad<u>ies</u>

Think About   What is the difference between a singular noun and a plural noun?

_____

_____

Read and Apply   Read the sentences. Put a line under each singular noun. Circle each plural noun.

Most foxes live in a forest or near a farm. But they

can also be found in the parks of big cities. A mother and

a father will make a home in their den. They feed their

pups and lead enemies away from the small babies. Some

farmers like the fox because it kills rats.

Write About Write some sentences about a wild animal that you like. Then circle any plural nouns you wrote.

_____

_____

_____

_____

_____

Review Read each singular noun. Write the plural form of the noun.

1. pony _____

2. cookie _____

3. glass _____

4. hat _____

5. watch _____

6. dish _____

Irregular Plural Nouns

Remember A **plural noun** names more than one. Sometimes you must change the noun to make it name more than one.

One	More than One	One	More than One
man	men	person	people
woman	women	foot	feet
child	children	mouse	mice

Sometimes the noun has the same singular and plural forms.

One	More than One	One	More than One
bison	bison	moose	moose
deer	deer	sheep	sheep
fish	fish	trout	trout

Think About Look at the first set of examples above. How did the nouns change to name more than one?

_____

_____

Read and Apply Read the sentences. Put a line under the nouns that name more than one.

   Many people enjoy visiting Yellowstone National Park. Men, women, and children will see something new. A person might see a tiny mouse or a huge bison. A moose stays by itself. Bighorn sheep live in a group. Sometimes two male sheep fight over a female sheep. People like to try to catch a large trout in a river. Never get too close to a wild animal. Stay at least 75 feet away from sheep, moose, and deer. Stay at least 300 feet away from a bear or a wolf.

26

Write About Look at the pairs of words in the boxes on page 26. Write six sentences. Use as many of these plural nouns as you can.

_____

_____

_____

_____

_____

_____

_____

Review Read these sentences. Look at the noun below each blank. Change the noun to name more than one. Write the noun in the blank. Use a dictionary if you need help.

1. The _____ have sharp _____.
              mouse   tooth

2. _____ were using _____ to make crafts.
        child   scissors

3. Some _____ caught _____ in the lake.
          man   fish

4. _____ fed the _____ by the pond.
      woman   goose

5. _____ can jump up to 12 _____ in the air.
     salmon   foot

Possessive Nouns

Remember A **possessive noun** names who or what has something. Add an **apostrophe** and an **s** to make a possessive noun. If a plural noun ends with an **s,** just add an **apostrophe.**

Noun	Ron	chickens
Possessive	Ron's glasses	chickens' food

Think About What punctuation mark do you use to make a noun possessive? Explain how to use it.

_____

_____

Read and Apply Read the paragraph. Put a line under each possessive noun.

A beaver's dam keeps the beaver safe. Beavers build dams in the water. The dam's door is under the water. Beavers use branches, logs, mud, and trees' bark to build the dam. Dams can be so big that they change the water's flow. Beavers have strong jaws and teeth. Beavers' jaws can cut down a thin tree in one bite! Beavers are hard workers.

Write About Write a paragraph about an animal's home. Use the possessive form of at least two nouns.

_____

_____

_____

_____

_____

Review Write possessive nouns to complete these sentences. Use the noun shown below the line.

1. The _____ bone is in the backyard.
           dog

2. The _____ den is over there.
           foxes

3. This _____ tire is flat.
           car

4. The _____ seats are by the window.
           women

5. Where are the _____ toys?
                      cat

6. Some _____ gloves are on the bench.
           players

Abstract Nouns

Remember An **abstract noun** names something that you cannot see, smell, taste, hear, or touch.

happiness	fear	childhood
truth	love	pride

Think About Look at these two nouns: <u>kitten</u> and <u>silliness</u>. Which one do you think is an abstract noun? Why?

_____

_____

_____

_____

Read and Apply Read the paragraph. Put a line under the five abstract nouns.

Safety is important when you ride your bike. First, be sure to wear a helmet. If you have trouble getting your helmet to fit, ask an adult. Secondly, know the correct hand signals to show where you are going. This helps avoid confusion. Car drivers know what direction you are turning. Always ride on the correct side of the road. Some websites give you more information about being safe on your bike.

Write About Look at the list of abstract nouns in the box. Write four sentences. Use a different abstract noun in each sentence. You do not need to use all the abstract nouns.

curiosity	bravery	trust	anger
trouble	loyalty	childhood	happiness
life	beauty	hope	love

1. _____

_____

2. _____

_____

3. _____

_____

4. _____

_____

Review Read each sentence. Put a line under the abstract noun in each sentence.

1. The teacher asked for silence in the room.

2. The soldier had a lot of courage.

3. Patience is important when painting a picture.

4. The puppy had a lot of energy.

5. Mrs. Stein taught her children good manners.

31

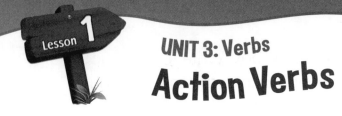

UNIT 3: Verbs
Action Verbs

Remember   An **action verb** is a word that tells about doing something.

climb   fill   baked   ran

Think About   The action verb <u>dance</u> tells about how someone or something moves. What other action verbs can you think of that tell about how someone moves?

_____

_____

Read and Apply   Read the sentences. Put a line under each action verb.

One cold morning in 1926, Gertrude Ederle dashed into the sea. She swam away from the French coast. Huge waves crashed and roared around her. Gertrude pulled and kicked through the rough water. Hours later, she reached England. Gertrude climbed out of the water.

Gertrude rode in a parade. People cheered for her. Newspapers printed Gertrude's story on the front page. Many people read about what Gertrude had done.

Write About Write a paragraph about something you would like to do. Then circle all the action verbs.

_____

_____

_____

_____

_____

_____

Review Write action verbs to complete these sentences. Use words from the box or think of your own.

| drive | toss | stand | clap | wave | laugh |

1. People _____ beside the road.

2. Colorful floats _____ past them.

3. The riders on the floats _____ to the people.

4. They _____ candy to the children.

5. The children _____ and _____.

Linking Verbs

Remember   A **linking verb** tells about being something. Linking verbs do not show action.

Linking Verbs   am   is   was   become
                 are   were   became

The students <u>were</u> late.

I <u>am</u> 9 years old.

Think About   How can you tell the difference between a linking verb and an action verb?

_____

_____

Read and Apply   Read the sentences. Put a line under each linking verb.

Glass frogs are small tree frogs. Their home is in trees in rain forests. A glass frog's skin is clear. Its heart and organs show through the skin. The frog's eyes are big. They are on top of its head. Male glass frogs become angry if other male frogs are near them.

In 2015, a new type of glass frog was identified. Scientists were in a jungle in Costa Rica when they discovered the frog. This glass frog is lime green, like other glass frogs. It is different from other glass frogs because it makes a whistle noise. It is also special for another reason. This frog looks a lot like the popular Muppet, Kermit the Frog.

Write About   Tell about an interesting animal. Circle any linking verbs you use.

_____

_____

_____

_____

_____

_____

Review   Write linking verbs to complete these sentences. Use words from the box.

am	is	are	was	were	become	became

1. I _____ excited for the party.

2. Abraham Lincoln _____ the 16th president.

3. The cookies _____ in the oven.

4. My shirt _____ still dirty.

35

Helping Verbs

Remember   A **helping verb** sometimes comes before the **main verb** in a sentence. The helping verb helps the main verb tell about doing or being.

Helping Verbs

is	am	are	was	were		
be	being	been	has	have	had	
do	does	did	will	shall	should	would
can	could	may	might	must		

The room will look cheerful.
↑ ↑
helping verb   main verb

Think About   How is the helping verb different from the main verb?

_____

_____

Read and Apply   Read the sentences. Put a line under each helping verb. Circle each main verb.

People have used knots for a long time. Bows and arrows were made by Native Americans with square knots. Sailors have tied knots for many years. Knots can hold sails in place. Knots might keep a boat from floating away. On a camping trip, strong knots will hold up a tent. Today, wire is taking the place of rope for some jobs. For other jobs, rope always will be the best tool.

Write About Tell about some ways that you have used knots. Use helping verbs.

_____

_____

_____

_____

_____

_____

Review Write a helping verb to complete each sentence.

1. Tony _____ sing well.

2. Everyone _____ drawn pictures.

3. People _____ standing in front of the door.

4. The dog _____ barking all night.

5. The band _____ play my favorite song.

6. A drink of water _____ taste good.

Present Tense

Remember A verb in **present tense** has two forms. Use the plain form with a plural subject. Use the s-form with most singular subjects. The subject and the verb must agree, or match.

Plural Subject **Monkeys chatter.**   Singular Subject **The monkey chatters.**

Add **es** to verbs that end in **s, x, sh,** or **ch.** If a verb ends in a **consonant plus y,** change the **y** to **i** and add **es.**

Plural Subject **Lights flash.**   Plural Subject **Airplanes fly.**

Singular Subject **A light flashes.**   Singular Subject **An airplane flies.**

Think About How can you make sure the subject and verb agree in a sentence?

_____

_____

Read and Apply Read the sentences. Put a line under the six verbs that are not in the correct form.

The 2016 Olympic Games begin in Brazil. Athletes comes from all over the world. They tries to do their best.

Simone Biles flips through the air. She land on her feet. She raises her arms in the air. Simone and her coaches watches the screen. The score appears. Simone win the gold medal in gymnastics! People call Simone the best gymnast ever.

The Olympic Games end. Team USA walks in the Closing Ceremony. Simone carries the American flag. The athletes wears their medals.

Write About Write a paragraph about something you do that makes you proud. Circle the plain forms of verbs. Underline the s-forms of verbs. Make sure the subject and verb agree.

_____

_____

_____

_____

_____

_____

Review Complete each sentence. Write the correct form of the verb shown below the line.

1. My dog _____ the cats.
              chase

2. The boys _____ in the pool.
                splash

3. A baby _____ loudly.
              cry

4. The outfielder _____ the ball.
                    catch

5. The horses _____ the water.
                drink

Future Tense

Remember Verbs tell when the action happens. **Future tense** means the verbs tell what will happen after right now. Put the helping verb <u>will</u> in front of the main verb.

Present tense **The captains shake hands.**

Future tense **Other players <u>will shake</u> hands.**

Think About How do verb tenses help you understand what you are reading?

_____

_____

Read and Apply Read the sentences. Put a line under the sentence that is not in future tense.

In the fall, people will plant bulbs in their gardens. Bulbs hold everything a flower needs to grow. They will grow into flowers in the spring. Over the winter, the ground will protect the bulb. The cold weather will keep the bulbs from growing. Spring will arrive. Then the bulbs will begin to bud. First, a green shoot will come out of the bulb. Then leaves will appear. Finally, the flowers will bloom. The bulbs will make more bulbs under the ground. This means more flowers will grow each year.

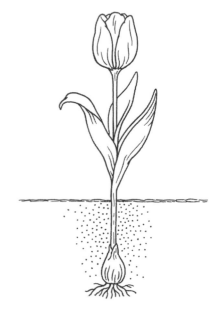

Write About Change these sentences. Write each one with the helping verb
<u>will</u> to make it tell about the future.

1. Watermelons come out in spring.

_____

_____

2. They begin as yellow flowers.

_____

_____

3. The big melons grow on long vines.

_____

_____

4. The vines hold the fruit in place.

_____

_____

Review Listen to each sentence. Circle **YES** or **NO** to show if the
sentence is in future tense.

1. YES   NO

2. YES   NO

3. YES   NO

4. YES   NO

5. YES   NO

6. YES   NO

Past Tense

Remember   Most verbs in **past tense** have a different form than in present tense. Add **ed** to most verbs to make them tell about the past. If the verb ends in **e,** just add **d.**

walk + ed = walk<u>ed</u>   like + d = like<u>d</u>

If the verb ends in a **consonant plus y,** change the **y** to **i,** and then add **ed.** If a short verb ends in a **consonant-vowel-consonant,** write the final consonant again and then add **ed.**

cry → cri + ed = cri<u>ed</u>   reply → repli + ed = repli<u>ed</u>

rub → rubb + ed = rub<u>bed</u>   snap → snapp + ed = snap<u>ped</u>

Think About   What do you notice about all of the examples above?

_____

_____

Read and Apply   Read these sentences. Circle the six verbs that are written incorrectly.

In the 1920s, Charles Drew hopeed to be a doctor. In those days, few African American people studied to be doctors. But Charles worked hard. He saved his money. He earned his degree.

As a doctor, Charles experimented with ways to store blood. He dried plasma. Then he useed it later for patients.

World War II startied. Hospitals needed blood. People donateed blood. They stored the blood in blood banks. The army shiped the blood to Europe. The blood saved soldiers in the war.

Write About   Write a paragraph about a person in history who did something special.

_____

_____

_____

_____

_____

_____

_____

_____

Review   Write the past form of each verb below.

1. paint _____   **5.** hurry _____

2. tie _____   **6.** nod _____

3. rest _____   **7.** smile _____

4. hum _____   **8.** cover _____

43

Past Tense: Irregular Forms

Remember Some verbs have a different spelling to show the past.

Present	see	come	do	go	grow	eat	give	know
Past	saw	came	did	went	grew	ate	gave	knew

Present	run	fly	take	begin	have	ride	sing	ring
Past	ran	flew	took	began	had	rode	sang	rang

Think About Do you see any rule in these examples? How do you think you learn these irregular forms of past tense verbs?

_____

_____

Read and Apply Read the sentences. Circle the correct form of the verb.

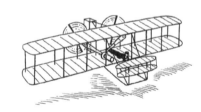

In Ohio in 1899, two brothers [have   had] an idea. They [began   begin] plans to build an airplane. They [did   do] experiments with kites and model planes. Then the brothers [go   went] to Kitty Hawk, North Carolina.

In 1903, the Wright brothers [take   took] their plane to a windy hill. Orville [fly   flew] first. He [came   come] back to the ground after 12 seconds. Next, Wilbur [rode   ride] in the plane for 59 seconds. Both brothers [see   saw] how their plane worked. They [know   knew] they had more work to do. But they were happy that the plane [ran   run] well.

Write About Write a sentence using the past tense form of the given verb.

1. eat

_____

2. give

_____

3. sing

_____

4. grow

_____

5. ring

_____

6. see

_____

Review Listen to each sentence. Circle **PAST** if the verb form is past tense. Circle **PRESENT** if the verb form is present tense.

1.   PAST   PRESENT

2.   PAST   PRESENT

3.   PAST   PRESENT

4.   PAST   PRESENT

5.   PAST   PRESENT

Forms of *Be*: Present Tense

Remember   The verb <u>be</u> can be a linking verb or a helping verb. It has different forms. Use <u>am</u>, <u>is</u>, and <u>are</u> to tell about the present. Use am with the word <u>I</u>. Use <u>is</u> with a singular subject. Use <u>are</u> with a plural subject.

I <u>am</u> collecting stamps.

This green one <u>is</u> my favorite.

The blue ones <u>are</u> more common.

Think About   How do you know which form of the verb <u>be</u> to use when you are writing?

_____

_____

Read and Apply   Read the sentences. Circle the six incorrect forms of the verb <u>be</u>. Write the correct form above the incorrect one.

It is New Year's Day in Philadelphia, Pennsylvania. People is waiting for the Mummers Parade to start. Mummers are people who dress up in costumes. The costumes is colorful and fancy. There are different kinds of mummers. Fancy mummers is the most beautiful. Comic mummers are funny. They do skits to make people laugh. A String Band mummer are a musician. The Mummers Parade is colorful and fun.

"I is excited to see the parade this year," says one parade watcher. "This am the best way to start the new year!"

Write About Write about a parade you watched. Write as though you are telling about it while you are watching it.

_____

_____

_____

_____

_____

Review Write the correct present-tense form of the verb <u>be</u> to complete each sentence.

1. I _____ at the parade.

2. The floats _____ driving past.

3. People _____ waving to me.

4. The band _____ playing a song.

5. Children _____ excited to see the clowns.

6. I _____ clapping for the dancers.

Forms of Be: Past Tense

Remember   The past forms of the verb be are <u>was</u>, <u>were</u>, and <u>been</u>. Use <u>was</u> with singular subjects. Use <u>were</u> with plural subjects. Use <u>been</u> with the helping verbs have and has.

Dr. Seuss <u>was</u> an artist and an author.

His drawings <u>were</u> on posters.

We <u>have been</u> reading some of Dr. Seuss's books.

Think About   What part of a sentence do you look at to decide what form of <u>be</u> to use?

_____

_____

Read and Apply   Read the sentences. Circle the six incorrect forms of the verb <u>be</u>. Write the correct form above the incorrect one.

Many cartoon characters was created by Walt Disney. Walt's first popular character was Mickey Mouse. Mickey were the star of many cartoons.

Walt were also interested in movies. The first movie he made were *Snow White and the Seven Dwarfs.* The movie was a hit! People have were enjoying cartoon movies ever since then.

It has was more than 80 years since Walt first drew Mickey Mouse. All Walt's characters have been favorites for a long time.

Write About Write a paragraph about one of the first movies you ever saw.
Circle forms of the verb <u>be</u>.

_____

_____

_____

_____

_____

_____

_____

Review Write the correct past-tense form of the verb <u>be</u> to complete
each sentence.

1. Disneyland _____ Walt Disney's dream.

2. It _____ built in Anaheim, California.

3. Many famous people _____ at Disneyland when it opened.

4. There _____ many problems on the first day.

5. Disneyland has _____ a popular place to go for years.

6. Mickey and his friends have _____ there from the start.

Perfect Tense

Remember   The words <u>have</u> and <u>has</u> can be used as helping verbs to tell about the past. They are used with the past form of most verbs. This is called **perfect tense.**

The fans **have stopped** talking.   The game **has started.**

Some verbs have a special past form to use with <u>have</u> and <u>has</u>.

Present	go	see	do	write	give	eat	begin	take
Past	went	saw	did	wrote	gave	ate	began	took
Special Past	gone	seen	done	written	given	eaten	begun	taken

Elena <u>went</u> to Mexico.   She <u>has gone</u> to visit her grandmother.

Think About   What words are clues that a sentence is written in perfect tense?

_____

_____

Read and Apply   Read the sentences. Circle the five incorrect forms of <u>have</u> or <u>has</u>. Write the correct form above each mistake.

People has visited the National Baseball Hall of Fame since it opened in 1939. The Hall of Fame have helped people learn about the history of baseball. People have seen pictures of players. They has read interesting stories.

Each year, the Hall have elected new people to the Hall of Fame. Not all the people have played baseball though. Some has written about baseball. Others have announced baseball games.

Write About Tell about a place you have visited as though you were writing in a journal.

_____

_____

_____

_____

_____

_____

_____

Review Complete each sentence. Circle <u>has</u> or <u>have</u>. Write the correct past form of the verb under the line.

1. Jayce [has   have] _____ to tie his shoe.
                          learn

2. Many people [has   have] _____ a falling star.
                                  see

3. Lila [has   have] _____ the last cookie.
                       take

4. The teacher [has   have] _____ the class a reward.
                                give

5. The men [has   have] _____ to fix the sink.
                            try

UNIT 4: Pronouns
Pronouns

Remember A **pronoun** is a word that takes the place of a noun. Use **subject pronouns** in the subject part of a sentence. Use **object pronouns** after action verbs and after words like <u>to</u>, <u>of</u>, <u>for</u>, <u>by</u>, <u>with</u>, and <u>from</u>.

Subject Pronouns	I	you	he	she	it	we	they
Object Pronouns	me	you	him	her	it	us	them

A pronoun goes with a noun. Make sure they agree, or match.

<u>Jim</u> paints <u>pictures</u>. <u>He</u> uses bright colors in <u>them</u>.

Think About How can you tell if a pronoun is a subject pronoun or an object pronoun?

_____

_____

Read and Apply Read the sentences. Put a line under each subject pronoun. Circle each object pronoun.

The first people to settle in Hawaii were Polynesians. They sailed to the islands in giant canoes. More Polynesians soon followed them. They made the Kingdom of Hawaii. It was ruled by a king and queen.

Kamehameha was Hawaii's first great king. He ruled all the islands by 1810. A holiday is named after him. It takes place in June. Liliuokalani was Hawaii's last ruler. She ruled it for just two years.

52

Write About Write about another leader. Tell something special about him or her.

_____

_____

_____

_____

_____

_____

_____

Review Complete the sentences. Write a pronoun to take the place of the words with a line under them.

1. Ed and Kathy went to the Fun House. _____ visited every room.

2. A talent show gives out prizes. Only the best performers win

   _____.

3. Juan saw a movie. _____ was very funny.

4. Mai did not feel well. Mom took _____ to the doctor.

Pronouns: *I* and *Me*

Remember I and me are the pronouns that take the place of your own name. I is a subject pronoun. Me is an object pronoun.

I walk to school with Erin.

Erin walks to school with me.

Think About How do you know when to use I and when to use me in a sentence?

_____

_____

Read and Apply Read the sentences. There are five mistakes with the pronouns in the sentences. Circle the mistakes.

I am learning to play piano. My teacher tells me to practice. She gives I music to play. First, me learned to read music notes. To some people, they look like dots. But me know that each note stands for a key on the piano. This helps me to play the music. Me learned to play scales. This means that I play notes in a certain order. There are different keys in music. Scales help I to learn more about music. Someday I want to play for many people. They will enjoy listening to me.

Write About   Write a paragraph about something you are learning to do.

_____

_____

_____

_____

_____

_____

Review   Write I or me to complete each sentence.

1. My dad and _____ built a birdhouse.

2. He showed _____ how to hammer in the nails.

3. Then _____ painted the sides.

4. Dad helped _____ hang the tree in the backyard.

5. Now _____ can watch the birds.

6. Dad points out different types of birds to _____.

7. He tells _____ more about each type.

8. _____ want to plant a butterfly garden next!

55

Possessive Pronouns

Remember   **Possessive pronouns** tell who or what has something.
Possessive pronouns do not use apostrophes.

my	your	his	her	its
our		their		

My brother and I rowed our boat.

He lost his oar.

Think About   How can you tell the difference between a pronoun and a
possessive pronoun?

_____

_____

Read and Apply   Read the sentences. Circle the possessive pronouns.

My family visited the National Aquarium in Baltimore.
The aquarium has eight dolphins in its dolphin exhibit. Their
oldest dolphin is Nani. Her children are Beau and Spirit.
Another dolphin is Foster. His mother is Jade. The dolphins
live together in their huge tank.

These dolphins are Atlantic bottlenose dolphins. Their
name comes from the shape of their noses. A dolphin's nose
is called its "beak." Dolphins use their beaks to look for food in
the sand at the bottom of the ocean.

I learned a lot about dolphins on our trip to the aquarium.

Write About   Write a paragraph about a trip you took with your family. Underline any possessive pronouns you use.

_____

_____

_____

_____

_____

_____

Review   Complete the sentences. Write possessive pronouns to stand for the words with a line under them.

1. Mrs. Richards watered _____ flowers.

2. The cat licked _____ paws.

3. We had a special visitor in _____ class.

4. Mike dropped _____ book.

5. Did you eat _____ sandwich?

6. The flowers lost _____ petals.

57

UNIT 5: Adjectives and Adverbs

Adjectives

Remember   An **adjective** is a word that describes a noun. It can tell how many, what color, what size, or what kind.

<u>two</u> shoes   <u>large</u> castle

<u>yellow</u> banana   <u>friendly</u> neighbor

Sometimes adjectives are before the noun they describe. Sometimes they are after the noun. They follow a form of the verb <u>be</u>.

I used the <u>sharp</u> knife.

The knife is <u>sharp</u>.

Think About   How do adjectives make your writing more interesting?

_____

_____

Read and Apply   Read the sentences. Put a line under each adjective.

Lewis Carroll wrote nonsense poems and stories. The funny poems and stories did not fit in real life. His most famous story is *Alice's Adventures in Wonderland.* Alice is a little girl. She follows a white rabbit down a deep hole. Then she finds herself in a strange world. There she meets a blue caterpillar, a crafty cat, and a mean queen. Alice is brave. She must find her way out of this unusual place. Then Alice wakes up. Was her weird adventure just a crazy dream?

Write About Write a paragraph about a funny story you have read. Use adjectives to give details about the story.

_____

_____

_____

_____

_____

_____

_____

Review Listen to each word. Circle **YES** if it is an adjective. Circle **NO** if it is not an adjective.

1.   YES   NO

2.   YES   NO

3.   YES   NO

4.   YES   NO

5.   YES   NO

6.   YES   NO

59

Articles

Remember   An **article** is a special kind of adjective. It signals that a noun will follow. The three articles are a, an, and the. Use a before a word that starts with a consonant. Use an before a word that starts with a vowel sound.

The divers scared an octopus.

It is a shy animal.

Think About   What type of word comes after an article? Is there more than one type of word that can come directly after an article?

_____

_____

Read and Apply   Read the sentences. Put a line under each article.

Sometimes a ship carrying oil has an accident. An oil spill in the ocean hurts many animals. If an otter or a bird gets coated with oil, the animal usually dies. People go to a spill to try to help the animals.

A veterinarian checks the animals. The workers use a special soap and water to clean the animals. The workers watch over the animals to make sure they are not sick. Then the animals are taken back to a clean area in the wild.

60

Write About Tell about an animal you have cared for. Use adjectives to make your writing interesting.

_____

_____

_____

_____

_____

_____

Review Use <u>a</u> or <u>an</u> to complete each sentence.

1. Do you want _____ banana or _____ apple?

2. Maria saw _____ notebook on her desk.

3. _____ alligator floated on top of the water.

4. There is _____ pencil on the floor.

Rewrite each sentence. Replace the articles <u>a</u> and <u>an</u> with the article <u>the</u>. Talk with a partner about how this changes the sentence.

5. A book is on a shelf.

_____

6. Kym brought a sandwich and an orange.

_____

Comparing with Adjectives

Remember   Adjectives can compare nouns. Add **er** to most adjectives to compare two nouns. Add **est** to compare more than two nouns.

long   long**er**   long**est**

If an adjective ends in **e,** drop the **e** and add **er** or **est.** If an adjective ends in **y,** drop the **y** and add **ier** or **iest.** If the adjective has one vowel before the last consonant, double the consonant and add **er** or **est.**

white   whit**er**   whit**est**

tiny   tin**ier**   tin**iest**

sad   sad**der**   sad**dest**

Think About   How do you know if an adjective is comparing two nouns or more than two nouns?

_____

_____

Read and Apply   Read the sentences. Circle the four adjectives that are wrong. Write the correct form or spelling above them.

There are four kinds of "big cats" in the world. Tigers are

the larger cats. They are longer and heavyer than lions. But lions

are taller than tigers. Big cats can roar. Lions have the louder

roar of all. The leopard is the smallest of the big cats. But it is

the strongeest climber. All big cats can run fast, but the tiger

and the jaguar are the fastest runners.

Write About   Write sentences that compare. Use the adjective and the form that are given.

1. shiny, compare three or more

_____

2. sweet, compare two

_____

3. green, compare three or more

_____

4. thin, compare two

_____

Review   Read each sentence. Circle the correct form of the adjective in parentheses.

1. This is the (funny) book I have ever read.

   a. funnyer   **b.** funnier   **c.** funnyest   **d.** funniest

2. I think kittens are (cute) than puppies.

   a. cutter   **b.** cuter   **c.** cuterest   **d.** cutest

3. Chloe used her (neat) handwriting.

   a. neatter   **b.** neattest   **c.** neatest   **d.** neater

4. Today is a (hot) day than yesterday.

   a. hottest   **b.** hotter   **c.** hotest   **d.** hoter

63

More Comparing with Adjectives

Remember Add a word before longer adjectives to compare nouns. Use <u>more</u> to compare two nouns. Use <u>most</u> to compare more than two nouns.

Describing Radio was an <u>important</u> invention.

Two TV may be <u>more important</u> than radio.

More than Two Computers could be the <u>most important</u> invention yet.

Some adjectives that compare are irregular.

Adjective	Two	More than Two
bad	worse	worst
good/well	better	best
many/much/some	more	most
far	farther	farthest

Think About How do you know which form of an adjective to use when you are comparing things?

Read and Apply Read the sentences. Put a line through the four mistakes. Write the correct word or words above each mistake.

Mary Pope Osborne thinks being a writer is the better job.

She visits the more exciting places in the world. She sees the

most beautiful sights. She travels farthest than many people do.

Mary travels through time, too. She is the author of the Magic

Tree House books. The characters go on the most wonderful

adventures. Some adventures are most difficult than others.

Some are more frightening. They are all fun!

Write About Tell what job you think is the best and why.

_____

_____

_____

_____

_____

_____

_____

Review Work with a partner. Read each sentence out loud. Rewrite the sentence. Correct the underlined adjective.

1. The chocolate cake is the <u>deliciousest</u> cake on the table.

_____

2. Today was the <u>most worse</u> day of my life.

_____

3. Right now, a marker would be <u>usefulest</u> than a pencil.

_____

4. Aunt Tina lives the <u>most far</u> away.

_____

Adverbs

Remember An **adverb** is a word that describes an action verb. It can tell how, when, or where something happened. Many adverbs end with the suffix **ly.**

How	Bailey paints <u>carefully</u>.
When	She finished a picture <u>yesterday</u>.
Where	Bailey hung it <u>downstairs</u>.

Think About What are some adverbs to describe something you did today?

_____

_____

Read and Apply Read the sentences. Put a line under each adverb.

Kudzu grows quickly. It completely covers trees and buildings. People brought this vine here from Japan. It grew well in the South. So people planted it in their gardens. The vine grew up the sides of houses. It shaded yards nicely. But it totally took over.

Now kudzu is a problem. People are slowly trying to get rid of it. They mow it regularly. They carefully use chemicals to kill it. People also try to control kudzu with sheep and goats. The animals gladly eat the kudzu for dinner!

Write About

Write about an experience you have had with plants or flowers. Use adverbs to tell how, when, or where.

_____

_____

_____

_____

_____

_____

_____

Review

Read each sentence. Put a line under the adverb. Then circle **HOW, WHEN,** or **WHERE** to explain what the adverb tells about the verb.

1. Dandelions grow everywhere.   HOW   WHEN   WHERE

2. The name "lion's tooth" fits this plant perfectly.   HOW   WHEN   WHERE

3. Dandelion leaves look exactly like sharp teeth.   HOW   WHEN   WHERE

4. Gardeners always hate to see a dandelion.   HOW   WHEN   WHERE

5. The plant's roots reach down three feet or   HOW   WHEN   WHERE
   more in the soil.

67

Comparing with Adverbs

Remember   Adverbs can show comparison. If an adverb ends in **ly,** make the comparison form by adding the word <u>more</u> or <u>most</u> before the adverb. If the adverb has the same form as an adjective, follow the same rules you use for writing the comparison form of an adjective.

Adverb	Two	More than Two
quietly	more quietly	most quietly
soon	sooner	soonest

Some adverbs that compare are irregular.

Adverb	Two	More than Two
well	better	best
badly	worse	worst

Think About   How do you know what form of an adverb to use?

_____

_____

Read and Apply   Read the sentences. Circle the correct form of the adverb.

Pythons move [more slowly   most slowly] than many snakes. They stay still for long periods of time. Then they move [faster   more fast] to catch their dinner. Pythons eat [rarelier   more rarely] than other snakes. Pythons may only eat four to five times a year!

Some people have pythons as pets. Pythons must be treated [carefullier   more carefully] than any other pet. It is [wellest   best] for pythons to stay in the wild.

68

Write About Write some sentences. Use a comparison form of the adverb that is given.

1. badly

_____

2. playfully

_____

3. near

_____

4. well

_____

5. loudly

_____

Review Listen to each sentence. Circle **TWO** if the adverb compares two actions. Circle **MORE THAN TWO** if the adverb compares more than two actions.

1.	TWO	MORE THAN TWO
2.	TWO	MORE THAN TWO
3.	TWO	MORE THAN TWO
4.	TWO	MORE THAN TWO
5.	TWO	MORE THAN TWO

Compound Subjects

Remember   Sometimes two short sentences have the same predicate. Join the subjects with the word <u>and</u> to make a **compound subject.**

<u>Hummingbirds</u> are tiny.

<u>Sparrows</u> are tiny.

Compound Subject   <u>Hummingbirds and sparrows</u> are tiny.

Think About   How can making compound subjects help you when you are writing?

_____

_____

Read and Apply   Read the sentences. Circle pairs of sentences that can be combined by making a compound subject.

Eagles are birds of prey. Hawks are birds of prey. A bird of prey is a bird that hunts for other animals. Eagles have very good eyesight. Hawks have very good eyesight. They can see their prey from far away.

Eagles are very large birds of prey. Hawks are medium-sized birds of prey. Sharp talons help birds of prey catch their food. Hooked beaks help birds of prey catch their food. Hawks eat smaller animals, like snakes and fish. Eagles can catch larger animals.

70

Write About Write a paragraph about one or two interesting birds. Write at least two sentences with compound subjects. Put a line under each compound subject.

_____

_____

_____

_____

_____

Review Read each pair of sentences. Write them as one new sentence. Use <u>and</u> to join the subjects.

1. Ducks can swim well.
Swans can swim well.

_____

_____

2. Ostriches cannot fly.
Penguins cannot fly.

_____

_____

3. Orioles build hanging nests.
Sunbirds build hanging nests.

_____

_____

Compound Predicates

Remember   Sometimes two short sentences have the same subject. Join the predicates with the word <u>and</u> to make a **compound predicate.**

Glass <u>is delicate</u>.

Glass <u>breaks easily</u>.

Compound Predicate   Glass <u>is delicate and breaks easily</u>.

Think About   How does using compound predicates make your writing more interesting?

_____

_____

Read and Apply   Read the sentences. Circle pairs of sentences that can be combined by making a compound predicate.

Glassblowing was invented thousands of years ago. People still do glassblowing today. Glassblowers mix ingredients. Glassblowers make hot liquid glass. The glassblower puts a pipe into the hot liquid. The glassblower blows into the pipe. The glass begins to form a bubble. The glassblower uses special tools to change the shape of the glass. The glass product is put in a special furnace. The glass product is slowly cooled. Then the product is finished. It is ready to be used.

Write About   Describe something you know how to make. Tell about how you make it. Use at least two sentences with compound predicates. Put a line under each compound predicate.

_____

_____

_____

_____

_____

_____

Review   Read each pair of sentences. Write them as one new sentence. Use and to join the predicates.

1. A glassblower uses special tools.
A glassblower has a very hot furnace.

_____

_____

2. The glass bubble stretches.
The glass bubble grows.

_____

_____

3. It comes off the tube.
It cools into hard glass.

_____

_____

73

Compound Sentences

Remember   When two short sentences tell about the same thing, they can be joined to make a **compound sentence.** Use the words <u>and</u> or <u>but</u>. Use a **comma** after the first sentence.

                         Becky has a cat. Ken got one, too.

Compound Sentence   Becky has a cat, <u>and</u> Ken got one, too.

                         Becky has a cat. Ken wants a dog.

Compound Sentence   Becky has a cat, <u>but</u> Ken wants a dog.

Think About   When would you use <u>and</u> to join two sentences? When would you use <u>but</u> to join two sentences?

_____

_____

Read and Apply   Read the sentences. Put a line under the three compound sentences. Circle the two sentences that you could combine to make a compound sentence.

The marimba is made of wooden bars, and it is played by hitting the bars with mallets. It was first made by African slaves in Central America. Now, a lot of Latin American music uses the marimba. Musicians usually play it with one mallet in each hand, but some musicians use two or three mallets in each hand. Some marimbas are very long, and two musicians can play them at one time. The marimba is the national instrument of Mexico and Guatemala. It is also popular in Africa.

74

Write About Write a paragraph about an instrument you would like to play. Include at least two compound sentences.

_____

_____

_____

_____

_____

_____

_____

_____

_____

_____

Review Use a comma and the word <u>and</u> or <u>but</u> to make a compound sentence with the two sentences.

1. The clarinet is a woodwind instrument. The trumpet is a brass instrument.

_____

_____

2. You play the piano with your fingers. You use drumsticks to play the drums.

_____

_____

3. The flute plays very high notes. Trombones and tubas play much lower notes.

_____

_____

75

Conjunctions

Remember   **Conjunctions** connect words and groups of words. The three most common conjunctions are <u>and</u>, <u>but</u>, and <u>or</u>.

Malik <u>and</u> Roger are on the soccer team.

Their games are after school <u>or</u> on Saturday mornings.

Malik will play again next year, <u>but</u> Roger wants to try baseball.

Think About   What words or groups of words does each conjunction connect in the examples above?

_____

_____

_____

Read and Apply   Read the sentences. Circle the conjunctions.

Misty Copeland was shy and scared at her first ballet class. Most ballet dancers start very young, but Misty was already 13 years old. She loved dancing and her classes. The American Ballet Theatre offered Misty a job, but first she finished high school. Then she started dancing with the American Ballet Theatre. At first, she danced small parts or in a group, but she dreamed of more. In 2015, Misty's dream came true. She became the first African American principal dancer with the American Ballet Theatre. Now, Misty wants to help boys and girls to get the chance that she did.

76

Write About Write a paragraph telling what you want to be when you grow up. Use at least two conjunctions in your paragraph.

_____

_____

_____

_____

_____

_____

_____

_____

Review Read the sentences. Circle the conjunction in each sentence. Put a line under the words or groups of words the conjunctions connect.

1. The ballerina wore a leotard and a tutu.

2. Is your dance lesson on Monday or Tuesday?

3. I am in the beginner class, but my sister is in the advanced class.

4. I must practice, or I will not get better.

5. Ms. Rodriguez and Miss Hoover are the dance teachers.

Complex Sentences

Remember   A **complex sentence** has two parts. Both parts have a subject and predicate. One part can stand alone. This part is called an **independent clause.** The other part needs the rest of the sentence to make sense. This part is called a **dependent clause.**

Mom took my picture after I finished the race.

↑   ↑

independent clause   dependent clause

Think About   How can you tell the difference between an independent clause and a dependent clause?

_____

_____

Read and Apply   Read the sentences. Put a line under the complex sentences.

No one had ever run a mile in less than four minutes. Roger Bannister wanted to be the first person to do it. Roger had a race on May 6, 1954. He almost did not run the race because the wind was blowing very hard. Roger decided to run after the wind calmed. People cheered when Roger crossed the finish line. The announcer said Roger's name. He started to say that Roger's time was "three minutes and…." The people did not hear the rest because they were cheering. Roger had done it. He was the first person to run a mile under four minutes.

Write About Write a paragraph about something you did that made you proud. Write at least two complex sentences.

_____

_____

_____

_____

_____

_____

_____

_____

Review Read each sentence. Put one line under the independent clause. Put two lines under the dependent clause.

1. I put the flowers in a vase after I picked them.

2. Tim helped Devin with his math because Tim understands fractions.

3. Mary closed the door when she brought the dog inside.

4. You cannot use the laptop if the battery is dead.

79

UNIT 7: Capital Letters

Proper Nouns and the Word I

Remember   Proper nouns begin with **capital letters.** The word I is also a capital letter. Holidays, months, and days of the week also begin with capital letters.

People	Mrs. Tanya A. Grimes		Dan
Animals	Rex	Little Beauty	American Pharoah
Places	Harvest Road	Kansas City	United States of America
Days	Wednesday	Fourth of July	Thanksgiving
Months	October	April	

Think About   Why do you think proper nouns use capital letters?

_____

_____

Read and Apply   Read the sentences below. Circle the letters that should be capital letters.

i visited the empire state building in new york city. This building is on fifth avenue in manhattan. The building is 102 stories high! william lamb designed the building. Workers began building the empire state building on march 17, 1930. It was the tallest building in the world for almost 40 years. The colors of the lights on the building can change. They are orange, white, and green for st. patrick's day. They are red, white, and blue for independence day.

Write About Write about a special place that you have visited. What did you learn about the place while you were there?

_____

_____

_____

_____

_____

_____

Review Write complete sentences to answer these questions. Be sure to use capital letters correctly.

1. What is your name?

_____

2. What city and state were you born in?

_____

Rewrite each word or group of words. Use capital letters correctly.

3. tuesday   _____

4. mr. ben smith   _____

5. new year's eve   _____

6. wood street   _____

Abbreviations and Initials

Remember An **abbreviation** is a short way to write a word. Usually a **period (.)** comes after it. If the abbreviation stands for a proper noun, it begins with a capital letter.

King Street	Monday	September	Doctor
King St.	Mon.	Sept.	Dr.

Abbreviations for states do not use periods. Both letters are capital letters.

Pennsylvania	New York	Florida
PA	NY	FL

An **initial** is the first letter of a name. It is a capital letter. Put a period after an initial.

Nicole A. Bell   J. R. Alvarez

Think About Why do you think the abbreviations for proper nouns use capital letters?

_____

_____

Read and Apply Read the sentences below. Circle the letters that should be capital letters.

Barack h. Obama became the president of the us on tues.

jan. 20, 2009. Obama is from Chicago, il. He was born on aug.

4, 1961 in Honolulu, hi. As president, Obama and his family lived

in the White House. It is on Pennsylvania ave. in Washington, dc.

Write About Write complete sentences to answer these questions. Use abbreviations when you can. Be sure to use capital letters correctly.

1. What is your full name? Use an initial for your middle name.

_____

_____

2. What is today's date? Give the month and the day.

_____

_____

3. Where is your school? Give the street, town, and state.

_____

_____

4. What is your principal's name? Give the principal's correct title.

_____

_____

Review Listen to each word. Write the correct abbreviation.

1. _____ 5. _____

2. _____ 6. _____

3. _____ 7. _____

4. _____ 8. _____

83

Beginning a Sentence

Remember   The first word of a sentence begins with a capital letter.

<u>W</u>hat is a ghost town?

<u>I</u>t is a place where no one lives now.

Think About   How might a capital letter at the beginning of a sentence help you when you are reading?

_____

_____

Read and Apply   Read the sentences below. Circle the letters that should be capital letters.

there are many ghost towns in the American West. people moved west. they were looking for gold. they built towns. sometimes they found gold. sometimes they did not find anything. the gold ran out. people could not live in the towns. they moved on to look for new places to live. soon there was no one in the town. then it became a ghost town.

Write About   Write a paragraph about what you think it would be like to find a ghost town. Underline the first letter of each sentence. Be sure to capitalize correctly.

_____

_____

_____

_____

_____

_____

_____

Review   Write the first word correctly to complete each sentence.

1. _____ ghost town is Bodie, California.
   one

2. _____ town was a mining camp.
   this

3. _____ came to the town to look for gold.
   people

4. _____ Bodie is a state park.
   today

5. _____ is full of things people left behind.
   it

Titles

Remember   The first word, the last word, and each important word in the **title** of a book or story begins with a **capital letter.**

Book   _Where the Wild Things Are_
Story   "Chicken Little"
Poem   "Casey at the Bat"

Think About   You learned that you use capital letters for proper nouns. How is using capital letters in titles the same?

_____

_____

Read and Apply   Read the sentences. Circle each word that should begin with a capital letter.

Katya is reading _grimm's fairy tales._ So far, her favorite one is "snow white and the seven dwarfs." She also enjoyed "cinderella" and "little red riding hood." Some of the fairy tales in the book are new to Katya. "the fisherman and his wife" is about a woman who always wants more. Next, Katya wants to read _the little mermaid and other fairy tales._ This book is by Hans Christian Andersen.

Write About   Write a paragraph to tell what some of your favorite books and stories are.

_____

_____

_____

_____

_____

_____

_____

_____

Review   Listen to each sentence about a book, story, or poem. Then listen to the title again. Write the title on the line.

1. _____

2. _____

3. _____

4. _____

87

UNIT 8: Punctuation
End Punctuation

Remember   Every sentence ends with a **punctuation mark.** Use a **period (.)** at the end of a statement or a command. Use an **exclamation point (!)** at the end of an exclamation. Use a **question mark (?)** at the end of a question.

Statement   Jonas was reading a book.

Command   Make something special for yourself.

Question   Do all plants need sunlight?

Exclamation   What a great night!

Think About   When might you use an exclamation point with a command? Can you think of an example?

_____

_____

Read and Apply   Read these sentences. Put the correct end punctuation at the end of each sentence.

Have you ever heard of the Seven Cities of Gold

The people of Mexico told stories about the cities

They were in a land called Cibola   How beautiful they

were   In the 1500s, Spanish explorers heard about

the cities   What do you think they did   They set

out to find the cities   Imagine what that trip was

like   What did they find   They looked for years

In the end, the explorers did not find the cities

Write About   Write each type of sentence. Use the correct end punctuation.

1. Write a statement of your own. Describe what a city of gold might look like.

   _____

   _____

2. Write a question of your own. Ask something more you would like to know about the explorers.

   _____

   _____

3. Write a command of your own. Think of something the Spanish leader might have said to his men.

   _____

   _____

4. Write an exclamation of your own. Tell something that you might say if you saw a city of gold.

   _____

   _____

Review   Read the sentences below. Fill in the circle next to each sentence that uses the correct end punctuation.

O What time does the movie start!   O May I see the picture?

O Tie your shoe.   O Sit on this chair?

O I would like to eat pizza.   O What a beautiful sunset!

O This tastes so good?   O My dog is brown.

89

Commas

Remember A **comma (,)** separates things. Use it between the day and year in a **date.** Use it between the name of a city and the name of a state.

Dates **June 14, 1952** **April 2, 2016**
Places **Atlanta, Georgia** **Billings, Montana**

Think About Where do you put the comma when you write a date?

_____

_____

Read and Apply Read the sentences. Add commas where they belong.

America's Civil War began on April 12 1861. It started at Fort Sumter South Carolina. The next big battle took place at Shiloh Tennessee. The worst battle was at Gettysburg Pennsylvania. The North and South fought for three days. The battle started on July 1 1863. The war finally ended on April 9 1865. It ended in the tiny town of Appomattox Court House Virginia.

Write About   Ask a partner the day and year he or she was born. Ask the city and state where he or she was born, too. Write two sentences telling the information.

_____

_____

_____

_____

_____

Review   Write each date or city and state name correctly. Put a comma in the correct place.

1. January 1 2017   _____

2. Albany New York   _____

3. May 19 2005   _____

4. Goose Island Oregon   _____

5. November 22 1992   _____

6. Williamsburg Virginia   _____

More Commas

Remember   Use a **comma (,)** after words like <u>yes</u>, <u>no</u>, and <u>well</u> when they begin a sentence. Use a comma after the name of a person to whom someone is speaking. The comma separates the word or name from the rest of the sentence.

No, David is not here right now.

Nathan, what kind of bird is that?

Use a comma before the words <u>and</u> or <u>but</u> in a **compound sentence.** It separates the two main parts of the sentence.

There are different kinds of bees, and each one has a job.

Think About   What is the comma's job in all of these examples?

Read and Apply   Read the sentences. Add commas where they belong.

"Raoul do you know who Franklin Chang-Diaz is?"

"Yes he was the first Hispanic astronaut. He was born in Costa Rica and then he moved to Connecticut. He did not speak English but he worked hard in school. Maria he went on seven space missions and he traveled to the International Space Station."

"Raoul is Franklin still an astronaut?"

"No he talks to people about taking care of the earth. He has also been in two movies and he has been on television shows."

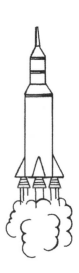

Write About Tell whether you would like to become an astronaut. Give reasons for your choices. Write your sentences as if you were "talking" to a friend. Be sure to include at least one compound sentence.

_____

_____

_____

_____

_____

_____

Review Write <u>Yes</u>, <u>No</u>, <u>Well</u>, or a person's name to complete each sentence. Use each choice once. Be sure to put the comma in the correct place.

1. _____ do some vets take care of farm animals?

2. _____ there are special vets for horses and cows.

3. _____ do people bring horses to a vet's office?

4. _____ the vet visits the horses on the farm.

Make the pair of sentences into a compound sentence. Be sure to put the comma in the correct place.

5. All vets need a lot of training. They have to like animals.

_____

_____

93

Commas in a Series

Remember   Use a **comma (,)** to separate items in a series.

Please buy milk, bread, and cereal at the store.

I ate a sandwich, chips, an apple, and some cookies.

Think About   Imagine writing a series of things without using commas. How could this be confusing?

_____

_____

_____

_____

Read and Apply   Read the sentences below. Put commas in the correct places.

The National Museum of Natural History has many interesting things. There are animals rocks and photographs. One area has items from Ancient Egypt. Mummies clay pots and jewelry help people understand life in Egypt. The dinosaur exhibit has fossils skeletons and pictures. The Ocean Hall is the largest exhibit. Visitors learn about whales fish giant squid walruses and jellyfish. There is a lot to see in the museum.

Write About   Write a paragraph to tell about a museum that you visited. Write at least one series of things. Use commas correctly.

_____

_____

_____

_____

_____

_____

_____

Review   Read each sentence. Fill in the circle next to the sentences that show all the commas in the correct places.

○   I had my books, pencils, and notebooks in my backpack.

○   The bake shop has cookies, muffins, cupcakes, cakes, and bread.

○   Mom grew, tomatoes corn, and green, beans in her garden.

○   Zoe saw monkeys giraffes tigers, and snakes at the zoo.

○   Be sure to pack your, toothbrush, comb, and pajamas.

○   Matsu speaks English, Chinese, and Spanish.

○   The art room has, crayons markers paintbrushes, and scissors.

Apostrophes

Remember An **apostrophe (')** can take the place of the letters left out of a contraction.

does not	we would	she is
doesn't	we'd	she's

An apostrophe is used to make a noun possessive. Add an apostrophe and **s** to make a singular noun possessive. Just add an apostrophe to make most plural nouns possessive.

Singular   doctor + 's = doctor's
a doctor's office

Plural   teachers + ' = teachers'
the teachers' meeting

Think About Explain two jobs of an apostrophe.

_____

_____

Read and Apply Read these sentences. Circle the apostrophes in contractions. Put a line under the apostrophes that are used to make a noun possessive.

Rainbows can't be seen unless there's both sun and rain. The sun's light bends as it shines through the raindrops. The light rays aren't all bending in the same way. Red light doesn't bend much. Violet light bends a lot.

Some people say you can find a leprechaun's pot of gold at the rainbow's end. That isn't true. It's only a story. Actually a rainbow doesn't have an end. A rainbow is really a circle. But we can't see the whole thing.

Write About Think of everyone in your family. What are their favorite colors? Write about them here.

_____

_____

_____

_____

_____

_____

Review Write a contraction for each pair of words.

1. we are _____

2. she would _____

3. he is _____

4. they will _____

5. is not _____

6. did not _____

Complete each sentence. Write the possessive form of the noun.

7. the _____ food
        cows

8. a _____ teeth
       tiger

9. _____ idea
      Mario

97

Writing Quotations

Remember   Conversation is what people say to one another. It is written in a special way. Use **quotation marks (" ")** before and after the exact words someone says. Use a **comma (,)** to separate the exact words from the rest of the sentence. The comma comes before the quotation marks. The exact words are like a sentence within a sentence. The first word begins with a capital letter. The end punctuation is before the last quotation marks.

Rita said, "I have never seen an owl."

Toby said, "An owl lives in a tree in my backyard."

Think About   What do quotation marks show you?

_____

_____

Read and Apply   Read the conversation. There are five mistakes in the conversation. Correct them using the proofreading marks.

Dante said "I saw a great horned owl at the nature center. They have other owls there, too."

Kim asked, Does a great horned owl have horns?

Dante said, "no, they have feathers that look like horns or catlike ears. They live all over America."

Kim replied "I would like to see one, but I live in a town "

Dante said, "You could still see one. They live in towns and in the woods. They hunt many animals, including skunks!"

⩔ ⩔	insert quotation marks
⋀	insert comma
⊙	add period
≡	capital letter

Write About   Write two conversation sentences of your own. Ask what a friend likes to see on a walk in the woods. Write the exact words you said. Write the exact words your friend said.

_____

_____

_____

_____

Review   Read the sentences below. Fill in the circle next to each statement that shows the quotation marks in the correct places.

○ Kate said, "We are going to the beach!"

○ "Jawon said," My bike has a flat tire.

○ "Suri asked, When is dinner?"

○ Denzel asked, "Is it raining outside?"

○ Emma said, "I like this song!"

○ "Xun asked," Have you seen my homework?

○ "Chula said, Let's play a game."

99

UNIT 9: Choosing the Right Word
Homophones

Remember   **Homophones** are words that sound alike, but they are spelled differently and have different meanings.

Their means "belonging to them." There means "in that place." They're is a contraction for "they are."

Their plan is to get there early. They're leaving at 5:30.

You're is a contraction for "you are." Your means "belonging to you."

You're sitting on your jacket.

Think About   What is a good way to figure out which homophone you need to use?

_____

_____

Read and Apply   Read the sentences. Find the four incorrect homophones. Put a line through each one and write the correct word above it.

Leonardo da Vinci and Michelangelo Buonarroti both came from Italy. They're art is in museums and buildings there. People travel from around the world to see their art. If your visiting the Sistine Chapel in Rome, you will see one of Michelangelo's greatest works. He painted the ceiling their. One of da Vinci's most famous paintings is the _Mona Lisa._ You must see these two great works with you're own eyes!

100

Write About   Use the given homophone in a sentence.

1. there

_____

2. their

_____

3. they're

_____

4. your

_____

5. you're

_____

Review   Circle the correct homophone to complete each sentence.

1. Rico and Ana ate [their   there] lunches at the table.

2. Do you want milk for [you're   your] cereal?

3. Let's sit on the bench over [they're   there].

4. [Their   They're] planning to build a new school.

5. When [your   you're] ready, please stand up.

More Homophones

Remember   **Homophones** are words that sound the same. They are spelled differently and have different meanings.

<u>Two</u> means "the number 2." <u>To</u> means "toward" or it is used with a verb. <u>Too</u> means "also."

Cameron brought <u>two</u> balloons <u>to</u> the party. He asked Aiko <u>to</u> bring balloons, <u>too</u>.

<u>Its</u> means "belonging to it." <u>It's</u> is a contraction for "it is" or "it has."

The dog left <u>its</u> bone here. <u>It's</u> going to eat the bone later.

Think About   How can you remember the difference between <u>it's</u> and <u>its</u>?

_____

_____

Read and Apply   Read the sentences. Find the five incorrect homophones. Put a line through each one and write the correct word above it.

The little penguin gets it's name because of its size. It's the smallest penguin. Little penguins lay two eggs at a time. The too parents take turns watching the eggs. A little penguin uses its two flippers to swim fast. Its shape helps it move quickly in the water, too. It swims and dives to catch fish. Its blue and white feathers are waterproof. Its able to stay warm in the cold water. Many people come two Australia and New Zealand to see little penguins. Those are the only two places too see one in its natural home.

Write About Use the given homophone in a sentence.

1. to

_____

2. two

_____

3. too

_____

4. its

_____

5. it's

_____

Review Circle the correct homophone to complete each sentence.

1. There are [two   to] bottles of water in the bag.

2. The cat was playing with [it's   its] toy.

3. Let's go [too   to] the park after school.

4. [It's   Its] time to go to bed.

5. I want to plant tomatoes and corn in the garden, [two   too].

6. I am going [too   to] ride my bike in the driveway.

Other Homophones

Remember **Homophones** are words that sound alike, but have different spellings and different meanings.

rode	road
deer	dear
blue	blew

Think About How can you make sure you are using the correct homophone when you are writing?

_____

_____

Read and Apply Read the paragraph. Circle the correct homophone to complete each sentence.

The United Nations works for [peace   piece]. This group has [bin   been] busy since 1945. At first, only the United States and 50 other countries [maid   made] up the UN. Now [there   their] are 193 members. The UN has [cent   sent] food and doctors to help people around the world. UN workers travel [through   threw] dangerous places to help people. The UN also has programs [witch   which] teach people the best ways to farm. The UN believes that everyone has certain [writes   rights].

Write About Look at each pair of homophones. Use each homophone in a sentence.

1. here/hear

_____

_____

2. ate/eight

_____

_____

3. knew/new

_____

_____

4. blue/blew

_____

_____

Review Read the sentences. Decide if the underlined homophone is correct. Write the correct homophone on the line if it is incorrect.

1. The grocery store has a <u>sale</u> on apples. _____

2. A <u>dear</u> ran past the tree. _____

3. This book is <u>buy</u> my favorite author. _____

4. Please put some <u>wood</u> on the fire. _____

5. Turn left at the next <u>rode</u>. _____

105

Naming Self Last

Remember   Always name yourself last. Use <u>I</u> as a subject. Use <u>me</u> as an object to answer what or whom after an action or with words like <u>of</u>, <u>in</u>, <u>to</u>, <u>for</u>, <u>at</u>, <u>from</u>, <u>with</u>, <u>on</u>, or <u>by</u>.

Kari and <u>I</u> jumped in the pool.

Mom watched Kari and <u>me</u>.

Bella wants to swim with Kari and <u>me</u>.

Think About   When you talk about yourself and two other people, where should you name yourself?

Read and Apply   Read the sentences. Circle the four mistakes in naming self last.

My family and me visited the Bronx Zoo in New York  City. It is one of the biggest zoos in the world. My sister and I loved the Children's Zoo. A mini Nubian goat came right up to my sister and I. We got to pet it. The zoo worker told my dad and I that the mini Nubian goat only gets about 2 feet tall. Dad and I liked the red goat the best. My family and I also saw the Butterfly Garden. Mom and me thought this was a neat exhibit. More than 12 types of butterflies live there. Finally my family and I went to the Madagascar exhibit. The lemurs made my sister and me laugh. They jumped around and swung on vines. They looked like they were having a fun time.

Write About Write a paragraph about something you enjoy doing with a friend or a brother or sister. Be sure to name yourself last.

_____

_____

_____

_____

_____

_____

Review Fill in the circle for the correct sentence in each set.

1. ○ Mom drove Liev and I to school.

   ○ Mom drove I and Liev to school.

   ○ Mom drove me and Liev to school.

   ○ Mom drove Liev and me to school.

2. ○ Chantal and I play soccer at the park.

   ○ I and Chantal play soccer at the park.

   ○ Chantal and me play soccer at the park.

   ○ Me and Chantal play soccer at the park.

3. ○ I and Dad rode the train.

   ○ Dad and I rode the train.

   ○ Dad and me rode the train.

   ○ Me and Dad rode the train.

107

Using *He* and *Him*, and *She* and *Her*

Remember   Use <u>he</u> and <u>she</u> as a subject. Use <u>him</u> or <u>her</u> as an object to answer what or whom after an action verb or word like <u>of</u>, <u>in</u>, <u>to</u>, <u>for</u>, <u>at</u>, <u>from</u>, <u>with</u>, <u>on</u>, or <u>by</u>.

<u>He</u> sat on the bench.   <u>She</u> is a singer.

The dog watched <u>him</u>.   I saw <u>her</u> on stage.

Then the dog sat next to <u>him</u>.   Micah sang with <u>her</u>.

Think About   Explain when to use <u>he</u> or <u>she</u> and when to use <u>him</u> or <u>her</u>.

_____

_____

Read and Apply   Read the sentences. There are six mistakes. Put a line through the incorrect word. Write the correct word above it.

John Adams was one of America's Founding Fathers.

His wife Abigail helped he. John was a leader in the new

country. He spent a lot of time away from home. Him

wrote to Abigail. Her wrote back to him. He asked she

what she thought about ideas. She gave him other ideas.

She also told him what people around she wanted from

the new country. Then John became president. Abigail

joined he in Washington, DC. She supported him as president.

John always wanted her to help him with his work.

John and Abigail Adams

Write About   Write a paragraph about two people who work well together. They can be real people or people you made up.

_____

_____

_____

_____

_____

_____

Review   Write the correct word to complete each sentence. Use one of the words under the line.

1. _____ listened to the song.
　　Her   She

2. Amber shared her snack with _____.
　　　　　　　　　　　　　　　him   he

3. _____ wants to learn to ski.
　　Him   He

4. The audience watched _____ dance.
　　　　　　　　　　　　her   she

5. _____ broke his arm.
　　Him   He

6. I asked _____ a question.
　　　　her   she

109

Using *We* and *Us*, and *They* and *Them*

Remember Use <u>we</u> and <u>they</u> as a subject. Use <u>us</u> and <u>them</u> as an object to answer what or whom after an action verb or a word like <u>of</u>, <u>in</u>, <u>to</u>, <u>for</u>, <u>at</u>, <u>from</u>, <u>with</u>, <u>on</u>, or <u>by</u>.

<u>We</u> went ice skating.

Ricky helped <u>us</u>.

He stayed with <u>us</u> on the ice.

<u>They</u> saw some birds.

The birds saw <u>them</u>.

The birds flew away from <u>them</u>.

Think About Explain when to use <u>we</u> and <u>they</u> and when to use <u>us</u> and <u>them</u>.

_____

_____

Read and Apply Read the sentences. There are six mistakes. Put a line through the incorrect word. Write the correct word above it.

Schools have changed over the years. We go to class with other children our age. A teacher teaches we math, reading, history, and science. Us also have classes like music, art, and physical education. Everyone goes to school. Some of we go to public schools. Some of us go to private schools.

Long ago, school was different. Children were together in one room. Them learned reading, writing, and math. They did not have many books. If children lived on farms, they did not go to school at all. Parents taught they at home. When them were 10 or 11 years old, many boys started to learn a job.

Write About   Write about an activity you enjoy doing at school. Do you think children long ago did this activity, too? Why, or why not?

_____

_____

_____

_____

_____

_____

Review   Circle the correct word to complete each sentence.

1. _____ parked their bikes by the library.
    They   Them

2. _____ want to go to the park.
    We   Us

3. Street signs tell _____ where to go.
        we   us

4. _____ went to see a movie.
    They   Them

5. Mrs. Carson made cookies for _____.
                they   them

6. Dad asked _____ a question.
        we   us

111

Writing a Friendly Letter

Remember

Letters are a way of talking to someone through the mail. A friendly letter has five parts. The **heading** is the writer's address and the date that the letter was written. The **greeting** says hello to the person who gets the letter. The **body** is the message of the letter. The **closing** says good-bye. The **signature** is the written name of the writer.

Use a **comma** to separate the city and state in the address. Use a comma after the greeting and after the closing.

Think About   Explain why the heading and greeting of the letter are important.

_____

_____

_____

Read and Apply   Read the letter. Label each part of the letter.

6 Apple Lane
_____ → Hershey, PA 17033
March 5, 2017

Dear Jose, ← _____

Please get well soon. We miss you at school. ← _____

_____ → Your friend,

_____ → Heather

Write About Write a friendly letter to someone you know. Tell him or her about something that happened to you this week. Include each part of the letter.

_____

_____

_____

_____

_____

_____

_____

_____

_____

Review Look at the letter in the Read and Apply section. Answer these questions about the letter.

1. Who is getting the letter? _____

2. Who wrote the letter? _____

3. Where does the writer live? _____

4. When was the letter written? _____

5. What is the letter about? _____

Addressing an Envelope

Remember Mail a letter in an envelope. The names and **addresses** of the person who wrote the letter and the person who is receiving the letter go on the envelope. Put a stamp in the upper right corner.

Person sending the letter }
Cliff Sandler
121 Overview Drive
Niles, OH 44446

Stamp →

Mrs. Martha Wong
29 Canyon Avenue
Butte, MT 59701
} Person receiving the letter

Think About How do you know which address the letter is going to and which address it is coming from?

_____

_____

Read and Apply Read the envelope below. Use the symbols at the right to correct the four mistakes. Circle the address for the person receiving the letter.

Michel Smith
135 West Market Street
Elizabethtown PA 17022

zach Chambers
73 park Street
Astoria OR 97103

≡ make capital letter
⋀ add comma

Write About Address this envelope. Use your name and address for the person sending the letter. Use your teacher's name and the school's address for the person getting the letter. Draw a stamp in the correct place.

_____

_____

_____

       _____

       _____

       _____

Review Look at the envelope below. Write the correct letter to show what goes in each spot. Not all the letters will be used.

A   B

C

D   E

1. Name and address of the person receiving the letter _____

2. Stamp _____

3. Name and address of the person sending the letter _____

Writing a Thank-You Note

Remember   A thank-you note thanks someone for a gift or for doing something special. Always name the gift or what was done and tell something special about it.

> 35 Rogers Street
> Bowie, TX 76230
> April 29, 2017
>
> Dear Mrs. Perez,
>
> Thank you for taking me to the water park with your family. The Rattlesnake was my favorite ride!
>
> Your neighbor,
> **Blake**

Think About   Why do you think it is important to tell what you are thanking someone for in a thank-you note?

_____

_____

Read and Apply   Read the thank-you note below. Put a line under the gift that the note is about. Circle what is special about it.

> 94 Wood Road
> Trenton, NJ 08608
> May 18, 2017
>
> Dear Aunt Clara,
>
> Thank you for the tickets to see *The Wizard of Oz* at the Harper Theater. It is my favorite movie, so I can't wait to see the musical. I am very excited!
>
> Your niece,
> **Lily**

Write About Write a thank-you note of your own. Thank a friend for a recent present or favor.

_____

_____

_____

_____

_____

_____

_____

_____

_____

Review Read the thank-you note below. Put a line through the information that is not needed.

104 South Aspen Avenue
Greeneville, TN 37616
February 21, 2017

Dear Uncle Marcus,

Thank you for the Valentine's Day card and candy. The card made me laugh. The candy was delicious. I don't like flowers.

Your nephew,
DeShawn

Grammar Handbook

Abbreviation a short way to write a word, usually ending in a period. Abbreviations for proper nouns begin with a capital letter.

> *Examples:* Jan.   Thurs.   Rd.

Abstract Noun a noun that you cannot see, smell, taste, touch, or hear

> *Examples:* friendship   loyalty   pride

Action Verb a word that tells about doing something

> *Examples:* think   leap   count   answer

Address the house number, street name, city, state, and zip code where a person lives

Adjective a word that describes a noun by telling how many, what color, what size, or what kind

> *Examples:* three bikes   tiny cat

Adverb a word that describes a verb by telling how, when, or where something happened

> *Examples:* run slowly   play today

Apostrophe a punctuation mark that takes the place of letters left out of a contraction or is used to make a possessive form

Article a special adjective that signals a noun will follow: *a, an,* and *the*

Body the main part of a letter

Capital Letter a large alphabet letter

Closing the part of a letter that says good-bye

Comma a punctuation mark that separates things or ideas

Command	a sentence that asks or tells someone to do something
Common Noun	a word that names any person, place, animal, or thing

> *Examples:* boy   park   cat

Complex Sentence	a sentence with two parts: a dependent clause and an independent clause
Compound Predicate	two predicates joined together in one sentence with the word *and*
Compound Sentence	two sentences joined together with the word *and* or *but*
Compound Subject	two subjects joined together in one sentence with the word *and*
Conjunction	a connecting word

> *Examples:* and   or   but

Date	a month, day, and year

> *Examples:* July 4, 1776   October 20, 2017

Dependent Clause	part of a sentence that has a subject and a predicate but does not make sense by itself
Exclamation	a sentence that shows strong feeling
Exclamation Point	the punctuation mark used at the end of an exclamation
Fragment	a group of words that does not tell a complete thought
Future Tense	form of a verb that tells about action that will happen later
Greeting	the part near the beginning of a letter that names the person receiving it

119

Heading	the part at the beginning of a letter that gives the writer's address and the date the letter was written
Helping Verb	a verb that helps a main verb tell about an action

Examples: <u>has</u> arrived   <u>is</u> sleeping

Homophones	words that sound alike, but are spelled differently and have different meanings
Independent Clause	part of a sentence with a subject and a predicate that makes sense by itself
Initial	the first letter of a name

Examples: <u>P</u>. <u>A</u>. Brown   Jerome <u>L</u>. Walker

Letter	a written message that is usually sent by mail in an envelope
Linking Verb	a verb that tells about being something, does not show action

Examples: is   were   are

Main Verb	the most important verb in a sentence
Noun	a word that names a person, place, animal, or thing

Examples: girl   school   kitten   sink

Object Pronoun	form of a pronoun that the action is happening to
Past Tense	form of a verb that tells about action that already happened
Perfect Tense	form of a verb that uses helping verbs to describe action
Period	the punctuation mark used at the end of a statement or command and most abbreviations

120

Plural Noun more than one person, place, animal, or thing

> *Examples:* trees benches children

Possessive Noun a noun that names who or what has something

> *Examples:* Jody's desk dogs' bones

Possessive Pronoun a pronoun that names who or what has something

> *Examples:* my shoes its tail

Predicate the part of a sentence that tells what the subject does or is

Present Tense form of a verb that describes action taking place now

Pronoun a word that can take the place of a noun

> *Examples:* she he it

Proper Noun a word that names a certain person, place, animal, or thing

> *Examples:* Ellie Nevada Fido *Mayflower*

Punctuation Mark a mark used to make the meaning of written words clear

Question a sentence that asks something

Question Mark the punctuation mark used at the end of a question

Question Word a word used to make a sentence a question

Quotation Marks punctuation marks used before and after someone's exact words in a written conversation

Run-On Sentence a group of words that tells more than one complete thought

Sentence a group of words that tells a complete thought and makes sense

Signature the writer's name at the end of a letter

Singular Noun   one person, place, animal, or thing

> *Examples:*   tree   bench   child

Statement   a sentence that tells something

Subject   the part of a sentence that tells who or what the sentence is about

Subject Pronoun   form of a pronoun that appears in the subject part of a sentence

Title   part of a person's name or the name of a book, story, or poem

> *Examples:*   Miss Brown   Dr. Sanchez
> *The Cat in the Hat*   "Cinderella"

USING CAPITAL LETTERS

- Begin every sentence with a capital letter.
- Begin each part of a person's name with a capital letter. Include titles that are used as part of the name and initials.
- Begin words that name days, months, holidays, and places with a capital letter.

USING PUNCTUATION MARKS

End Marks

- End every sentence with a period (.), a question mark (?), or an exclamation point (!).
- End a statement with a period.
- End a question with a question mark.
- End an exclamation with an exclamation point.

Commas

- Use a comma before the joining word in a compound sentence.
- Use commas between words that name things in a series.
- Use a comma between the day and year in a date.
- Use a comma between a city and state.

Apostrophe

- Use an apostrophe to show who owns or has something. If the owner is singular or is a plural form that does not end in **s,** add an apostrophe and **s.** If the owner is plural and ends in **s,** add just an apostrophe.

Quotation Marks

- Use quotation marks before and after the exact words a person says.

SHOWING TITLES

- Capitalize the first word, last word, and every important word in a title.

- Underline book titles

- Use quotation marks for shorter works, such as poems and articles.

USING CORRECT GRAMMAR

Subject-Verb Agreement

- When you use an action verb in the present tense, add **s** or **es** to the verb if the subject is a singular noun. Do not add **s** or **es** to the verb if the subject is plural.

- If the subject is a pronoun, add **s** or **es** to the verb only if the pronoun is *he, she,* or *it.*

Subject-Verb Agreement with Forms of *be*

- If the subject is a singular noun, use *is* for the present tense and *was* for the past tense.

- If the subject is a plural noun or more than one noun, use *are* for the present tense and *were* for the past tense.

- Use the correct form of *be* with a singular or plural pronoun subject.

Present Tense		Past Tense	
Singular	**Plural**	**Singular**	**Plural**
I am you are he, she, *or* it is	we are you are they are	I was you were he, she, *or* it was	we were you were they were

Irregular Verbs

- Many past tense verbs do not end in **ed.** It will help to learn the correct forms by heart.

Present	Past	Past Participle
is	was	(has) been
begin	began	(has) begun
bring	brought	(has) brought
choose	chose	(has) chosen
come	came	(has) come
go	went	(has) gone
have	had	(has) had
know	knew	(has) known
make	made	(has) made
run	ran	(has) run
say	said	(has) said
take	took	(has) taken
write	wrote	(has) written

Subject and Object Pronouns

- Pronouns have different subject and object forms.
- Use subject pronouns as the subject of a sentence.
- Use object pronouns after an action verb.

Subject	Object
I	me
he	him
she	her
we	us
they	them

Naming Yourself Last

- When you speak of yourself and another person, name yourself last.

125

NOTES